Hedgehog is hungry

Story by Beverley Randell
Illustrated by Drew Aitken

2

Winter is here.

4

Hedgehog is asleep.

Spring is here.
Hedgehog wakes up.

Here comes Hedgehog.

Hedgehog is hungry.

Here is a snail.

Hedgehog is hungry.

Here is a worm.

Here is a caterpillar.

Here is a beetle.

Here is a slug.

Hedgehog is hungry
in the spring.